BOA
EDITIONS LTD

Mandatory Evacuation

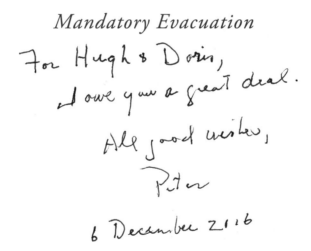

For Hugh & Doris,
I owe you a great deal.

All good wishes,
Peter

6 December 2116

*BOA wishes to acknowledge the generosity of the following
40 for 40 Major Gift Donors*

Lannan Foundation
Gouvernet Arts Fund
Angela Bonazinga & Catherine Lewis
Boo Poulin

Mandatory Evacuation

poems by
Peter Makuck

AMERICAN POETS CONTINUUM SERIES, NO. 158

BOA Editions, Ltd. ❋ Rochester, NY ❋ 2016

First Edition
16 17 18 19   7 6 5 4 3 2 1

For information about permission to reuse any material from this book please contact
The Permissions Company at www.permissionscompany.com or e-mail permdude@
gmail.com

Publications by BOA Editions, Ltd.—a not-for-profit corporation
under section 501 (c) (3) of the United States Internal Revenue
Code—are made possible with funds from a variety of sources,
including public funds from the Literature Program of the National
Endowment for the Arts; the New York State Council on the Arts, a
state agency; and the County of Monroe, NY. Private funding sources
include the Lannan Foundation for support of the Lannan Transla-
tions Selection Series; the Max and Marian Farash Charitable Foun-
dation; the Mary S. Mulligan Charitable Trust; the Rochester Area
Community Foundation; the Steeple-Jack Fund; the Ames-Amzalak Memorial Trust in
memory of Henry Ames, Semon Amzalak, and Dan Amzalak; and contributions from many
individuals nationwide. See Colophon on page 104 for special individual acknowledgments.

ART WORKS.
arts.gov

State of the Arts

NYSCA

Cover Design: Daphne Morrissey
Cover Photo: *Hurricane Watch* by Sherryl Janosko
Interior Design and Composition: Richard Foerster
Manufacturing: McNaughton & Gunn
BOA Logo: Mirko

Library of Congress Cataloging-in-Publication Data

Names: Makuck, Peter, 1940-, author.
Title: Mandatory evacuation : poems / by Peter Makuck.
Description: First edition. | Rochester, NY : BOA Editions, Ltd., 2016.
Identifiers: LCCN 2016019622 (print) | LCCN 2016024006 (ebook) | ISBN
    9781942683186 (pbk. : alk. paper) | ISBN 9781942683193 (ebook)
Classification: LCC PS3563.A396 A6 2016 (print) | LCC PS3563.A396 (ebook) |
    DDC 811/.54—dc23
LC record available at https://lccn.loc.gov/2016019622

BOA Editions, Ltd.
250 North Goodman Street, Suite 306
Rochester, NY 14607
www.boaeditions.org
A. Poulin, Jr., Founder (1938–1996)

For Phyllis

my first reader and so much more

and

For Bruce Bennett

with thanks for his insightful suggestions

Days are where we live—Philip Larkin

We remember moments, not days—Cesare Pavese

Contents

III. Tattoo

– I –

NOTES

Picnic near St. Rémy

These roadside poplars
in a long line
daub us with shade.
Wild poppies
the French call *coquelicots*
dot the high meadow grasses.
To our left a footpath
curves out of sight
leading to ladies
in long dresses,
parasols held overhead—
the bliss
of La Belle Époque.

Our blanket arranged
on new grass,
wine uncorked, we break
a baguette
and like ripping canvas
the sky shears
with six jet fighters
flying low.

Colors darken.
We plug our ears.
We wince.
We wait for Renoir-time
to return
its impossible sweetness
a long time gone.

Notes

Sunset spreads like a bloodstain
above this Spanish town, this overlook café.
You put down your pen and look around,
everything withering into words, but so what?

The narrow gorge now lives in your notebook
where dozens of swifts and kestrels will flare
again, swerving between the cliff walls
far below. Even that moment when a drunk

saw you peering over the edge and told you
women jump here, men over there,
laughing in your face through his wild beard
before he staggered away down the cobbles.

This is Ronda, one of the *pueblos blancos*
Hemingway used in a novel. The gorge,
deep at almost 400 feet, divides the town
and you imagine what happened to captives,

darkness seeping into the air you breathe.
A bent woman in black climbs step by step
to the church. A thin orange cat
eases along a wall that edges the drop.

Your coffee is gone. A bus starts up
and slowly groans across the bridge.
In a still moment, you pick up your pen
and from the other side comes a trumpet,

wavering phrases of a melody remembered,
the Aranjuez concerto, and the world
is reduced to those notes rising
like strange birds in the late orange light.

Orthodox Priest

Black cassock hiding his feet,
    he drifted onto the terrace
of this hillside café with its view
of the Laconian bay full of sunset,
and took me from politics at our table
to dim orthodox churches

and chapels of the last two weeks,
    to ikons and frescoes,
those wide eyes of saints and scribes
that resurrected my altar-boy moments
of flickering candles, holy oil, incense,
    and echoing quiet.

Our talk tacked like sails on the bay
as I watched him alone at the railing,
gold crucifix at his chest, long gray beard,
    kamilavka crowning his head.
Far below were red-tile roofs, shadows,
    the snares of everyday passion.

Turning from the rail, he passed our table
    and looked down on me
from those ikons, frescoes, and vaults—
reminders of sheer silence, thin places,
caves, hermits, and monasteries
    high in the mountains.

Table talk returned to my ears. Cats
    at my feet meowed for a handout.
Our talk was politics again
until loud voices and laughter had me turn
    to a table where the priest
now sat with the owner and his friends.

Leaning back in his chair, legs crossed,
fine Italian shoes exposed,
    he was smoking a cigarette,
arguing politics, and drinking ouzo,
    just like me.

Burro at Christmas

This jenny watched me lean against the fence
from the far side of the pasture.
When I dangled my hand with a carrot nub,

she slowly plodded my way, stopping to rip
some grass, taking her time. The first nub,
she lipped from my palm and crunched

allowing me to scratch her ears, pat her
smooth gray flanks with those dark lines
that legend says were left by the legs of Christ.

With the second carrot I was elsewhere,
thinking maybe about a Bible story. She bit
and shook. My finger came back bleeding.

My fault, not hers, still sweet as ever.
"A love bite," said my wife as I applied
a bandage, "but that might leave a mark."

　　　Or a lesson about presence:
When you feed the burro, just feed the burro.

Après Ski

Barefoot, I hobble over pebbles
pushing through icy snow.

Steam lifts a tattered curtain
from a hot tub on the hotel's roof.

Below the treeline,
white arteries come branching down

carrying nothing now
through lodgepole and piñon,

the last patrol sweep done.
The stars blink on.

A misty couple, already immersed,
laughs and gazes at the sharp white peaks.

I pause to make it last, then sigh
into the hot water with them,

sink into the pleasure of an image,
the tight grip of a scene.

Entry for San Carlos, 12/28

All afternoon on dusty dirt roads—
empty, except for a hunter's pickup
that passed us with a buck's head

and huge rack, its eyes open,
staring over the tailgate. Then
empty desert again: prickly pear,

spreads of ocotillo, sage flats, sharp
lines of mountains getting closer.
Two scurrying roadrunners

and one javelina
as we rumbled over a cattle guard.
What else? Corralled horses,

one distant ranch house,
a water pump windmill, and finally
in front of a tarpapered shack

in all this emptiness
rose a huge hand-painted sign:
Don't Talk Too Much About Yourself!

Good advice—but I wasn't
and am still trying not to.

Roadside

A 12-gauge propped on his hip,
one guard in sunglasses watches from the tree shade

this line of men in state-issue orange
working with grass-whips at ditch weeds,
full swings,
as if they are limbering up,
practicing for that golf course they'll never see.

Signs

In front of back-road country churches
signs that say

        COME IN FOR A FAITH LIFT
or
        JESUS CARES

or a few miles further

        OUR BOSS IS A JEWISH CARPENTER.

Then stopped at the crossroads
by Buzzard's Corner Grocery
        a sticker on the tailgate
of a rifle-rack pickup waiting for the light:

        JESUS LOVES YOU . . .

And the much smaller print
        you inch forward to read:

          . . . but most folks think
          you're an asshole.

Red Foxes at Pahaska Tepee

In an isolated no-frills cabin
on the banks of the Shoshone,
we spent two nights on the site
of Wild Bill Cody's hunting camp,
but unlike Bill, I had no gun
   to discourage the bears.

Make noise when you walk the trails,
they told us at the office,
and don't go into the woods after dark.

As a kid growing up in the country,
I read about Cody,
   Crockett, and Boone,
had a pistol and two rifles,
hunted rabbits and squirrels for the table,
trapped muskrat, fox, and mink for the money,
often missing the bus into school.

Behind our cabin one morning,
I spotted five deer
and a fawn feeding among the aspens.
At first I thought they were shadows.
   A few minutes later,
my binoculars brought a fox up close,
black forelegs and white-tipped tail.

I couldn't stop watching her
down on a path by the riverbank.
I'd never seen one playfully roll in the dust,
or stretch out while her two kits
   nipped at each other,
and tumbled over their mother.

Years ago
        when I saw a fox
it was held in the jaws of my trap—
five bucks bounty from the farmer's grange,
another buck and a half for the pelt.
        Who was I?
What was I doing?
I must have imagined I was Crockett.
What stays
from one of those mornings
is a red fox, bloody foreleg tight in my trap.
She was just standing there panting
with her tongue out
like my good dog Jonesy on a hot day.

But now as I watched, she jumped up,
this red fox mom,
        looked right at me, frozen,
flanked by her two kits.
I was dangerous,
I didn't deserve this gift of seeing.

Something stirred in the bushes beside me.
When I looked up again and tried to refocus,
they were gone,
                the riverbank empty.

Canyonlands in October

We hiked into the Flutes
over a dry wash full of flickering mica,
        up through sage, rabbitbrush
and Mojave aster, those tiny lavender petals.

At a red rock cliff face,
we stood before Fremont petroglyphs
        a thousand years old: bighorn sheep
and sentinel aliens with wide-apart fingers.

Later it was Castle Rock,
Sheets Gulch, Sandy Mesa, Studhorse Peaks.
        And that one dead juniper—
a black sculpture, limbs twisted against the sky.

At night, still sorting images,
I opened the door and stepped into a silver dark
        on the deck of the desert cabin
old friends let us take for a week.

No car sounds, no lights,
just distance, and a sky full of lurid stars,
        a low moon outlining
a jagged peak called the Cockscomb.

Like a symphony, the land drops
and surges in an upwash of scrub
        to bench or hillcrest without a sound,
but with a want of words to tame

        the vastness in all directions.
My yes-no argument came alive again.
        I just stood there, waiting for a sign,
something to take for a yes. Nothing.

Then two yips and a howl
from a distant high slope on my right.
          The cold quiet seemed to listen.
Off to my left, from the night's dark throat

          an answer of yips and a long howl.
Feeling like an early human, I just stood
          and listened to this back and forth, listened
to their need for talk and song,

          memorizing as much as I could.
I wanted to wake you, have you listen too,
          but I had to stay still,
keep that howling *yes* alive in my ears.

Now

A wrong turn in a new town.
An old neighborhood, azaleas and purple plum.

Warm afternoon.
Stuck behind a school bus with flashing lights.

You're late, but relax.
Something worthwhile might arrive.

Lower the window.
An orange meniscus lifting in the east. Not bad.

A young woman
waits at the side of the street with folded arms.

A small boy
jumps off the bus, his red backpack

flickering in the tree shadows.
He runs to his mom, and grabs her hand

years ago—your son, your wife.
The cars behind you begin to beep.

Wisteria sweetens the ripening light.
That wrong turn now seems right.

Jumping Mullet

You kill the outboard,
let the echo settle,
lean back on the gunnel.

On the slick black face
of Tranter's Creek,
peace in magnification,
water that barely idles:
droplets from oar tips,
the flash
and splash of mullet
trying to leap free
of what makes them itch.

Let the creek be
        what it is,
a place where nothing
much happens,
some backwater of the mind
where you find
all the nothing you need.

The water sleeps
and a trance takes
hold of the trees,
hold of the water,
leaf and silence,
silence and self
the same.

Book Barn

(Niantic, Connecticut)

With an armful of possible buys,
looking for a place to sit,
to finalize,
I move along the aisles,
an armchair at the end of each,
all occupied,
                    then spot an empty
but before I can reach it,
one of the barn's many cats,
                    an old gray,
jumps up,
curls down,
and pretends
deep sleep.

What Color Does

The screen door opening
frames a lizard
on a stretch
of unpainted railing,
a drag strip
where this anole,
green as a new leaf,
blinks,
then burns away down the track
slowing to a stop
at the porch roof column
where he turns
to the near pewter
of weathered wood,
nearly vanishes
like varnish,
taking me with him.

Night Passage

On the last jet leg
of a long flight home,
Kyoto temples still vivid,
I could hear
the monks chanting,
see stone lanterns, sculpted gardens,
the curl of smoke from joss sticks
flavoring the air.

But I was losing
to what came from a seat behind me
several minutes after the pilot said
to turn off all cell phones—
a kid in a loud fight
with his distant mother,
telling her she didn't
know shit.

With no ear bud music,
just a book
about Zen to calm me,
I finally stood up,
leaned over
and told this kid
with green hair,
rings in his nose and lips,
to shut it, right now,
or I'd call the flight attendant,
told him that I
and others around him
had not paid to listen
to this disrespect for his mother.

When I sat back down,
a woman in the next seat
touched my arm
and said thanks. But Kyoto
and its temples were gone.
Triple-tiered pagodas,
rock gardens, deep quiet,
monks, incense,
the Buddha—
gone.

Practice

When you open the living room drapes,
stand for a while with coffee in hand. Watch

titmice and chickadees fluttering
in first light at your feeder on the deck.

Then sit on the floor by the glass door.
Assume the posture. Breathe deeply.

Let silence absorb the swish-pass of cars.
When the winter sun tops the live oaks,

moves across the deck and into the room,
you need only watch the good tidings

of warm light that inch across the
rivering grain in the hardwood floor

finally warming your feet. Let it seep
into your pores deeply, feel it flow

in your veins. Tell yourself you need
no more than you have. Close your eyes.

Visualize the face of the bronze Buddha
that sits on your desk. Whisper, *Home,*

then repeat it with a soft final *Thanks.*

Winter

after Andrew Wyeth

It begins in the cold studio room
windowing the blank expanse of Kuerner's Hill,
his father not long in the ground.
This boy comes running,
a dark brown apparition, one arm drifting free,
the other frozen, an erratic figure
pitched down the steep mound of earth.
No sky or clouds, no high colors.
The summer blue of pie berries forgotten.
Only thin sunlight to blacken the turf
with a long shadow
stuck like flames to his fleeing heels.

It will be winter now, always
a process of separating muted color
from the earthdark his father has become—
dun and ochre, gray and black,
the whites all cold.
No Frenchy greens or reds,
just murky firs, a dull brick farmhouse wall,
a blue barn door,
a geranium like an ember in the woodstove dark.
Even in the summer of *Christina's World*
it is winter, grasses of the long rise
parched and bleached, the woman sprawled
in a pink so faded it's nearly white, abandoned

like this boy—earflaps wild in the wind.
He is crossing
the ghost tracks of a farm truck
that climb the hill past patches of snow,

fence posts, bare brush fringing the top
toward that deadly crossing hidden on the other side
where trains still wail without warning.

– II –

BARRIER ISLAND

Barrier Island

The lighthouse beacon reaches
across the moon-streaked ocean to our upper deck.
I'm soaking up the quiet,
the repeated phrases of waves,
the onshore breeze on my sun-burned skin.
You make not a sound coming out,
so my breath stops
when you touch my back, as if an avenger
had come to heave me over the railing.
For a few minutes you hug me goodnight,
then drift away to our bed
as the soft rap rap
of a Coast Guard chopper gets louder.
I watch it follow the shore, stop
and hover half a mile out,
its spotlight searching the swells.

One summer-school night in Québec
after drinking at a dive called the Chien d'Or,
I smuggled Renée into my room.
Three floors up on a narrow street
in the Quartier Latin,
we did what we wanted,
and afterward joked about our Jesuit professor.
With peerless memory,
Renée could recite Baudelaire, whole poems,
but one line comes back—
Je veux creuser moi-même une fosse profonde—
because after beers on another night she told me
about her mother's death,
her father's whores,
her brother jumping from the Pont de Québec.

In the morning, I woke up squinting
at a sun shaft slanted through the open casement.
She was gone.
A breeze ghosted in the gauzy curtains.
From the cobbles below came
the clip-clop echo
of a horse pulling tourists
toward the sights of Basse-Ville.
I went to the window.
The walkway was empty below.

Years later
at a language conference,
Monique, a mutual friend,
told me Renée had twice married and divorced,
lost a teaching position to drink
and ended as barmaid in a beachfront grill.
Early one morning a jogger
discovered her purse
and neatly piled clothes on the sand.
Days later,
her body came up in a fisherman's net.

The helicopter's gone
but not the long reach of moments
no barrier can stop,
arriving like the beacon's light
that finds me so easily across the years,
a swimmer caught in a riptide
of his own making
until I leave the deck
and turn my back
on the spotlight moon in our casement.
At bedside, I pause over your peaceful sleep
then try the same for myself
but lie awake
and watch the fan blades turning above us.

Mandatory Evacuation, Late August

Maybe
you'll be lucky.
You trailer your skiff to a storage lot.
Now drive with the ocean on your left,
building but still sunny,
surface a wide plane of glitter.
You'd never know what was coming
       and once upon a time
nobody did—sometimes dead-on surprise.

You pull into a pier lot for a last look.
Ten-footers rolling in with some surfers
and your friend's line:
The only people who welcome this weather
       are surfers and looters.
Two laughing gulls on the shed roof
       cracking up
as if they were put there to mock you.

On the way home to load the car,
you think about leaving
with a few family photos then see
at the roadside a mama raccoon with two kits,
her radar sensing what's on the way
and looking for a good place
to hunker.

Maybe nothing, you tell yourself.
It happens almost every year on this island.
The ocean heating up.
Maybe something temporary.
You'll be back in no time, maybe.
A few days from now.
Your house still standing.
Maybe.

After Hurricane Earl

When police reopened the bridge
        and let us back on the island,
there was a low orange sun in the east,
a gift assortment of clouds on the move.
No branches, trees, or power lines down,
no shingles missing as expected,
no roof leaks, ruined carpets
and furniture,
        but the beach was different.

The low tide sand was crowded,
not with bathers—
not a single person in sight—
but with hundreds of tires,
some peppered white with barnacles,
broken loose by the surge
from offshore artificial reefs,
the whole scene looking like a Magritte,
a limbo of lost dark souls,
or the work of teenage pranksters—
I couldn't say which. I just looked
at the absence of pattern
disappearing in the distance,
and down at the great company names
now barely readable:

Bridgestone   Goodyear
                Cooper
                        Eagle
Firestone
        Wrangler . . .

But I'd been facing west,
and up the beach behind me idled
three high-sided trucks
followed by men in orange
jumpsuits from the county jail,
        tossing up tires
to their workmates in the truck beds.
One of them grinned and said *Hey,*
so I asked him how it was going.
        He laughed
then yelled that it beat the hell
out of another day in the slammer,
his buddies now laughing too.

I watched them move down the sand,
        turn into silhouettes,
heaving tires against the sun,
and thought that today,
maybe only today,
we had all lucked out.

Gone

Walking through maritime forest,
he tops the ridge dune, beach empty,

ocean blue as the ink of her last letter,
that perfect nun-schooled cursive,

this last aunt, gone with family
stories that should have more deeply

needled his heart. Afternoon shadows
thicken in the white sandy hollows,

sea oats at his back and far out
a sharp line that divides two worlds.

He is thinking of a Polish uncle escaped
from Nazis when, as if sent by a deity,

appears a woman in a blue wetsuit.
She drags a red kayak out through the wash,

hops in, and paddles out
to the eight footers that

tip her over and send her back
boiling in a white seethe to the sand.

At last she finds her feet, staggers
and retrieves the kayak. Again

she launches out and again goes upside
down in the loud pound of the surf zone.

All this emptiness but for sandpipers
that suddenly rise, as if with one will,

twist and head in a new direction,
then swirl down a hundred yards east.

When he looks back
the red kayak is beyond the breakers

in a field of sun sparks pointed west, slowly
appearing and disappearing far from shore.

Power Outage

The room goes dark.
Candles become the evening news,
three wavering tongues

telling about stillness and
that bright moon in the window.

Out of Range

Tourists were gone, and the last
bronze beauty in a two-piece had vanished.
          Mornings were colder.
I walked to the dock with a bucket
of fish heads, feet finally echoing on wood,
water rippling against boats in their slips.

The sky was a blank mind,
pulling blue from a remembered Monet.
          Then I saw it, a great black
shadow in the channel, breaching
with a gust of breath by the dock's end.

My first thought was *dolphin*, common
in the Carolinas, but this was a manatee.
          I said *manatee*
just for the fun of its sound and got
what I had never expected. Slowly,

she swam to my dangling hand and
let me scratch her head, just like a dog.
          White barnacles speckled
a black back dashed with scars,
likely from boat props. Huge flippers,

wrinkled skin, tiny wide-apart eyes,
and a fat whiskery snout.
          When this ugly beauty submerged
a herring gull stalled above me.
Then silence turned up its volume

broken by the whine
of a daysailer's pump. A minute later

            a guy on the next dock
was yelling, pointing. When I got there,
she had a bilge tube in her mouth,

drinking all the green water
that flowed from the bottom of his boat.
            "She must be a vegan,"
we joked, but finally refueled, she looked about,
and submerged for the last time.

Back at my crab trap, re-baiting
and shaking blue shells into a bucket,
            I refused her a risky future,
imagining her final approach to Florida waters
surfacing to breathe new color and light.

Nightcatch

When the green tail shrimp
thicken in Bogue Sound in October,

let your skiff drift along the edge
of the channel at four or five feet.

Make it a still night with a moon,
or maybe Orion bright overhead,

smooth black water at your feet.
Now sling that lead-weighted web.

Watch it spread wide and ploosh,
dozens of shrimp flash in all directions

like a starburst, except those that thump
and flicker inside of your net coming up.

Release the choke, let them snap
and bounce on the deck, their bodies

translucent. Throw back the smalls,
jumbos in the cooler. Hold one up.

Wonder at the black bead eyes on stalks,
a green moon on each tail blade.

Take your time. Let the quiet magnify.
When you lift the hem of your net,

ready for the next toss, allow yourself
to leave the moment for a second—

a few more nights like this, you'll have
hundreds headed and veined, bagged

in the freezer, enough to take you
all the way to next summer.

Yellow Chair in the Dunes

With rusty joints, collapsible,
forgotten, it's a *memento mori* of sorts,
a reminder of how soon
you become blind to the place
where you live
and why you visit
this walkway that crosses the dunes
to become a gazer again
        at the blue-green water.

All through summer, a woman,
slim, blond, and attractive,
would sit in a black two-piece
between the dunes
        in that yellow chair
beneath an umbrella with her dog,
always reading a novel.
A widow, some say.
Clouds billowed offshore
and surfers rode the big waves in
but she rarely looked up.
When she went for a swim
her golden retriever went too
until she told him to stay
and he would lie above the tideline
keeping close watch.

For weeks she's been gone.
The chair keeps its vigil, aimed
at a gray-haired man
who walks from the beach toward the dunes,
sweeping the arm of a metal detector.
        He could be your double,

looking for what's lost,
always hoping to leave here with gold.

Towhees and Late Light

You could almost miss them
on, among, or half under leaves
fallen from oleander and oak,
these quit-less hunters
of cutworms and bugs,
    digging, kicking leaves
        and wood chips a few feet out
onto our concrete drive,
sun low and close
to the tint of their rusty sides.

I think of you,
lost to death for a whole year now,
but still a presence
like this bright waver of light
reflected from the birdbath
onto the front room wall.
I'm watching the tremble
of light and your favorite birds.

To live for the eye,
you once said,
is to be on to something
and you always were.

A sunshaft flares
across the drive, then dims.
The dark begins its slow descent,
but that light on the wall
still wavers, and will

long after it's gone.

In Advent Dark

Just weeks ago before he died
a neighbor I knew but slightly
put out at the end of his pier
an electric tree—red, yellow, green.

I've been taking after-dinner walks
and love its look from Pelican Point
or the dune path to Fiddler's Ridge,
how it hovers above the black water.

On freezing nights, I still go out
to see it, the day's trivia fading fast
before his isosceles aglitter with gems,
making me wish I could thank him.

Tennis Courts in December

Cold three early mornings in a row. And gray
as those three headless doves on the fence, trees

a black weave of branches. Not a single
cardinal with a bright offering. Just the green

surface of the tennis courts across the distance
from this window. For a year at least,

an elderly man has been inside the fence
every morning with his old golden retriever.

His blue Jeep by the gate. Both limping along,
he checked his watch at the end of each lap

around the twin courts and stayed no matter
what the weather until he'd clicked off twenty-five.

The retriever tried to stay close but hobbled behind
for a lap or two, then lay near the net, tracked him

with her eyes, and thumped her tail as if in applause.
It ended with him opening the hatch of the Jeep

and her putting both front paws on the tailgate.
Then he'd lift her haunches, shut the hatch,

and disappear down the street. Next day,
in his red cap, they'd reappear for a rematch,

refusing to be beaten, emptiness kept at bay,
all of us winning that old game of space and time.

It's now been two weeks since I've seen them.

Outer Banks Nightlife

You wake in the dark
to the outside light triggered on.
Raccoon you first think, but now
     a fox with black legs,
          a sly red
out by the porch
     that begs
you to follow
     his fading into a ditch
          that edges the yard

back into a darkness
     now lit as never before.
Your breath plumes white.
     You sniff for a thread
          of scent
from vole, rabbit, or better
     away from car noise
where the less wise finish
     as roadkill.

This ditch takes you past a house
     where a man stands
before the altar
     of his flickering TV
          (drink in hand)

then into an understory
     of vine, catbriar,
          and wax myrtle.
Holly leaves gleam
     in slim beams of starlight.

Cold glazes your face
        but you don't mind,
brush snagging your hair,
        scraping your cheeks
as you move on all fours
        toward the regular inhale
and exhale of surf.

Under live oaks and loblollies
        you stand in a chill quiet.
Barred owls
        hoot hi-lo's
            back and forth
across the distance.
        Pine scent.
            Gems of sap
along the starlit bark.

You slip past rabbit bones,
        a scatter of fur,
            and emerge at last
from the cover of trees
        where bright freed stars
            fall into place.

Far down the beach,
        a motel spotlight
            shines out to sea,
hundreds of gulls in its long beam
        glittering like confetti.

Fixative

Winter nights, after dinner, I go out
into the dark, hoping for something bright
to hold the day. I take the salt marsh path
that leads to the wide waters of Bogue Sound.

Sometimes I return with a wash of stars
in my head. Or the antiphonal hoots
of Barred Owls that have built their sound fence
in hi-lo's for maybe a mile. Tonight

there were no stars. A cottony mist hung
over the trees like a tent. Just a soft slapping
of waves at the point. But on the return,
from the road in front of my house, I heard

a panic of squeaks in the pampas grass.
My flashlight lit the cats, Mel and Tootie,
tormenting a mouse that they left by turns,
coming to my feet for strokes and scratches

until the mouse escaped—likely to our shed
where the lucid dark of my desk lamp
shows him still, entering this room from a hole
in the wall, uncertain at first, sniffing

left then right, as if looking for a switch.
But that's me, not him, looking for a light.
He scurries for birdseed to the torn sack,
then burrows to sleep in my garden glove.

Flu Days

Shivering, you drag yourself,
as if gun-shot, to the living room,

to the old movie channel,
to a Bogart festival,

your mind fogged over
(like the street on the screen)

edging toward feverish sleep
when Bogey snarls

at Ida Lupino:
"Of all the 14-carat saps . . ."

Hours later when you wake,
he's smacking Peter Lorre:

"When you're slapped,
you'll take it and like it!"

And as if cuffed, you black out,
head pounding, and come to

upon Ingrid Bergman
and "You must remember this,"

before fading again, then back
to Bogey hacked to death

by Bedoya's machete,
all that gold dust blown away

with the whole bloody day,
everything gone—gone black

as your living room windows—
those previews of The Big Sleep.

Held

I was almost home
when into the headlights ran
a raccoon, then stopped.

Those thuds and what the rearview
held made their way home as well.

Blue Beyond Black and White

East as usual
on Hooker Road
then west on Gilead
toward the end
of a three-mile run
and the sun hit
my face
with needle wind
from the plowed field
all sea-gulled white,
those hidden hundreds
that suddenly rose,
broke the field
into fluttering
black scraps
like burning bits
of paper,
the air torn
with cries where
they churned
and flapped above
me puffing
to a stop, breath
a white delight
when they
settled deep
as snow again,
and the sky
was blue
beyond the help
of any words.

Wisteria

When the trees reach a gauzy green
before peak leafage, it begins to appear

dangling down like a nest for some
fantastic bird, ten to thirty feet above

ground, color ranging from purple
to a light lavender, unseen for a year.

And if the color doesn't pinch attention,
its fragrance will, filling your car

on that first warm day when you drive
with windows down on a country road.

Some cluster like bunches of grapes,
or hang like light-blue lanterns left

by someone who knows we need them,
or swaying censers, their sweet balm

filtering inward, making everything new.

Coastal Java Shack

I decide to clock out,
stop at this waterfront bistro
I've driven past dozens of times,
carry a steaming dark roast
                    to the window,

"Chronic Blues"
on the house speakers,
                    Coltrane
keeping me
from the lockbox of thought.

I sink into the soft swallow
            of an armchair
at the edge of a room
            quiet with people
staring at laptops,

and stare at a sailboat
            on its low-tide side.
But what makes me focus
            are two pigeons
that land on the dock planks
            a few feet away—
                    flying rats,
        or *shit birds*
some people call them,
but a bird
                    that can roll a 360
            to escape the plunge
of a peregrine.

With every step,
they cock their heads
                better to see.
Pinkish red feet,
        orange eyes
with a black dot at the center,
their necks
        a shiny iridescence.

In bird books
        they're "rock doves,"
                and I'm seeing
        the two homers,
Penny and Phil,
I kept as a kid
in a loft atop our garage.

I released them once
at my grandfather's farm.
They circled, then flew
                the twenty-five miles,
        making it home
before we did
in my father's new Ford.

        I'm there and here
at the same time,
        clocked out,
just watching the pigeons.

– III –

TATTOO

Tattoo

O Death, where is thy sting?—I Corinthians 15:55

It might have been June, on the back porch,
a few weeks before I sold my parents' house.

It's hard to remember exactly, or honestly.
What first looms into view is a sweating glass

of ice tea on the white table. Maybe I watched
the ice cubes melt and shift. Soaked with sweat,

I was drinking what he did when finished. The lawn
I had just mowed for the last time stretched

away to the gray stonewall where woods began.
The scent of cut grass must have been strong,

the west going amber, but what were my thoughts?
Years have buried them. I'll guess I was checking

for those cut corners Dad called "holidays"
and would make me drag out the mower to fix.

A wasp drifted into my line of sight, legs dangling,
like the arresting hook on a carrier jet. And that might

have led to the fighter pilot uncle I never knew, or
the gray globe of a nest hanging from an oak limb.

What brought back the moment was a faint tickle.
I looked down. It appeared on my forearm

like a vivid tattoo. A three-section body, thin waist,
long abdomen curved and tipped with a wet sliver.

Years ago I'd have quickly flicked it like a spitwad
at Joe Gaffney across the aisle in high school. Instead

I must have been seeing my father, one of his tricks.
He'd snag a wasp in midair, shake it inside the ball

of his cupped fingers, then put it on his arm.
We'd watch the tail flex, the stinger sink.

He'd laugh, blow it off, and warn us not to try.
Now it was my turn. House empty behind me,

I watched the wasp bend its abdomen.
Wherever my mind had been, that barb brought it back.

The green woods pulsed. A crow cawed.
The yard, porch, and moment throbbed,

needled itself inside me to find at last
a way out, the ink now dry, absence piercing as ever.

Mother's Day

In cap and gown,
valedictorian of her high school class,
        quicksilver smile—
this is the photo that helps me forget
sharp words between us,
her clouds of cigarette smoke,
the organ music of afternoon soaps,
and her cup holding more than coffee.

But let me turn back
to an afternoon I was grounded,
supposedly hunched over homework.
Through the air vent I could hear her
on the phone downstairs, talking—
not about the arrow I shot into Dickie's leg
but a petition that was snaking its way
through our white neighborhood of Slavs,
Irish, Jews, and Italians.
No blacks.

I stared
at a galaxy of pinholes
in the green window shade,
at the pull cord with its crocheted ring
dancing in the breeze, as I'd be dancing
and wincing for that accidental arrow
        when my father got home.
Then I heard my mother say *Manson*.
A name I knew well—Gary Manson.
He was black, my Little League teammate,
who'd eventually set records in track.
Gary.

When the shade
huffed out again, there was Mrs. DeNoto,
dressed in her church hat and heels,
strutting up the walkway
with a clipboard pressed to her chest.
The doorbell chimed.
        I heard mumbling,
then my mother quite loud: *Dolores,*
I know what it is,
and I will never sign it, never.
        The door slammed.
Everything was quiet, a different quiet,
as if an angel had passed.

Finally I heard
the scratch of a wooden match.
Across the varnished hallway floor,
I slid on my belly to the balusters.
Mom was lost in an armchair,
almost hidden in smoke—first time
I had ever seen her with a cigarette.
Forget the arrow, I prayed,
but she didn't,
and my father did what he had to.

But one of my mother's best moments
is the one with Dolores DeNoto,
though some neighbors shunned her
after the Mansons moved in.
Gary became one of our gang.
We had baseball in the street,
bike races, Tarzan swings
in the woods.

A year after she died,
my father, at seventy-two,

got punched in the face.
A mugger was kicking him
in an alley behind the bank when
who should rush from the shadows,
drop the guy,
then hold him in a headlock
until the police arrived,
but Gary.

Coincidence?
Sure, if you want it that way.

Petunias on the Deck

Even petunias are dying in this cold.
For days I've watched them
in a terra-cotta pot
curling up their red and white capes,
nodding, defiantly opening
for a few hours in the afternoon,
as if, near this final freeze,
they could go on forever. Before he died,
I trimmed my father's toenails
but in the process cut his toe,
made him see red,
list my history of fuck-ups,
and how his back door still needed fixing.
But before I could buy the new hinges
he was lying in a casket
below the tears of family and friends,
where I tried to fix things with a eulogy
that kept breaking down.

       Once in sunset light,
we walked our drinks
to a bench by the ocean,
listened to the light slap of waves,
and watched pelicans crash dive
into a school of bluefish,
coming up comically empty.
He looked at me and we laughed.
The sky was busy with clouds.
The water had a deep satin shine.
It was a pure moment
full of gleam and color,
wordless and unfiltered
as this red clay pot
and the raw throbbing of petunias.

Streetlamps

The last long streaks of sunlight
finally slip
from photo cells
atop each pole
and one, two, three
down the hill
above the brick street and yellow leaves
it begins—
not the soft white
hovering and shimmering I saw
those grade school nights
on bedroom ceiling and wall,
but a harsh, almost purple glow.
They're not angels any more
but keep
a kind of faith
(flicker though it will)
with my parents' house,
the woodstove kitchen,
the music and voices
drifting upstairs
to my room,
keeping the dark
at a distance.

The Route

Getting up before dawn was easy then.
On our porch, I'd wait until up the street
came my father with a truck full of milk.

He'd slow down so that, running, I could grab
the outside grip and swing myself inside
with the clinking glass bottles. The truck was

a Divco you could drive standing up,
its white sides saying *Farm Fresh Milk* in red.
Dad had my breakfast waiting in a bag

from Ed's Diner, egg and bacon on a bun
that I'd wash down with a half pint of cold
chocolate as we headed off on the route.

He taught me how to use the hand carrier
on snarly dogs when I went through gates
onto porches, some bottles with cream

risen to the top like a layer of pale gold
waiting to be found at first light. Few words
passed between us except for the orders

of cream, chocolate, skim, or "homo"—
homogenized, which made me laugh
not quite knowing why. We also laughed

about a collie that tagged us from street
to street and kept dropping a golf ball
on the truck floor until I'd pick it up

and fling it onto a dark lawn thinking
he'd never find it, but he always did.
I loved being on the road before dawn,

excited about the next thing to come
out of the dark, never tired or worried
until the sun rose and my father's last

delivery was me. At school, I'd scuff
into a dim world of nuns in black habits
where I'd watch the clock and pigeons

on top of the church roof, waiting for them
to hit the air and take me on another route.

Parish School

In a burning black lake of asphalt,
        next to the granite church,
it seems to be sinking,
        tilting in layers of heat.

Slung with camera and lenses,
        I work my way past
a concrete Virgin grottoed against
        the embankment, and crouch

to foreground the rusty incinerator,
        twists of smoke that took
our letters to Mary, black scraps
        rising to heaven as we sang,

"How dark without Mary
        life's journey would be,"
watching Sister Rosa's directing hands
        swoop like white bats.

Longshot: three stories of faded brick,
        Victorian trim, windows glary,
black firestairs Z-ed to the wall.
        By the time I enter, I'll be

a child again, halls immense as ever,
        the basement still dark
where the older boys would drag you
        through the stink of piss

and shove your head in the toilet.
        The cracked mirror where
I combed my wet hair still holds my face
        but there isn't enough light

for a reading. Barely more upstairs
             where a nun tidies her desk
and stands where I ask her, by a blue chart
             for Lenten Mass Attendance,

by wilting flowers in a cut-glass vase
             that gathers and condenses
what light there is. I can already see her
             shadowy face, sad and lean,

rimless glasses enlarged, evolving
             on matte paper in my dark room
with a huge dead Jesus above her.
             I wonder if students still kneel

for Penance, if prayers are still said
             for the conversion of Russia,
if, before First Communion, she still teaches
             the children their sins.

My answer rehearsed, I want her to ask
             if I still go to church
but feel instead as if kept-after again,
             knuckles rapped with a ruler,

to solve impossible problems in math,
             to let X equal all the bitter images
ever developed in this room.
             "Thank you, Sister,"

I find myself saying and wonder why
             as I drive away with the rattle
of her beads in my skull and all the stills
             I could ever hope to get rid of.

Footstool and Mug

Morning coffee defogs the deck.
I'm looking out,
just gazing at pansies that sway
and lean from a red clay pot
      on the footstool
my father made in his shop.
Ages ago.
Then it hits me
I'm drinking from the mug
with glazed blue tulips
a potter friend made for my mother.
Silence brightens.
My mother was a reader.

My father was a maker.
At his red vise,
he'd stand me on a soda crate
to drill through pencil dots
on slabs of pine, angled
perfectly with a miter box.
Then I'd screw together
a birdhouse or footstool,
and sand rough edges away,
him saying
"Good, good" as I went.

Both pansies and tulips
help something come back
      from the dark.
They brighten their colors.
Now I know what they want.

Names

My father, recovering from surgery
before TVs were the hospital room norm,
said, *Listen, I'm paying for your education.*
      Get me something good to read.

In college then, I first tried Hemingway
      on this Polish auto mechanic.
On my next visit, he said,
      This is baby talk,
and did an imitation that made me laugh.

So I told him Einstein thought
      The Brothers Karamazov
was the best novel ever written.
      Fine, he said, *I'll give it a try.*
And loved it—the only novel he ever read.

At our garage, under a car
with a grease gun, I overheard him
once ask a customer/teacher,
      Have you ever read . . .
then describe Fyodor, the horny old buffoon,
Dmitri in a troika madly hunting Grushenka . . .

Again spending time with the Karamazovs,
I realize this morning
that with names and nicknames
      Russian and Polish come close.
Names so hard for my students
posed no problem for my father,
for in Babcia's farmhouse kitchen,
pet names for my cousins, uncles,
and aunts swooped about

like exotic birds: Vanka, Vlad, Lidka.
And for me too: Piotr,
        Piotrek, Petrush,
Petruska, and more.

Developing Story

From the hillside framed in his window
he looks back to the keyboard,
this young father at his alcove desk.

His wife is off shopping in town, his son
napping downstairs, the house quiet.
Everything forgotten but those mountains

he has never seen, and that imagined
back-country skier, alone, in the deep
drifting snow, struggling to be found . . .

until the house-quiet turns up
its uneasy volume and hurries him down
to the bedroom, the bed rumpled and

empty. He yells the small boy's name
to the dining room, living room, bath and
kitchen—all empty, the screen door open.

Jesus, please begins another story
in this hill country pulsing with cicadas,
pulling everything from his mind

but the barn and sheds that are empty,
this tall grass he should have mowed
a month ago, tall enough to hide a . . .

Shouting, he's now a character, his own,
the whole story unimaginably real.
He yells again, then tells himself to listen.

The empty fields rage with cicadas. No one
to help on this remote hilltop chosen
to help him toward all the right words.

He runs down the slope toward a forgotten
dump site, past a pile of rattlesnake rubble,
and wind in the leaves of the poplars

is whispering good news: the boy's there,
amid cans and broken bottles by a fridge
with a wide-open door and black sealing lips.

Soaked and breathless, eyes stinging,
he now feels the weight of more
than a son riding high on his shoulders.

The crickets are scolding him back
to a different house, the boy laughing,
kicking, and yelling, "Giddy up, giddy up!"

Miss Jones

wasn't my teacher,
but maybe she was in a way,
a small whitish mongrel
with one floppy ear
I can't remember
not having
nights at the foot of my bed.
On school days,
according to my mother,
she'd be asleep
on our front porch glider,
wake at 3:10
and cross the street
to meet my bus at 3:15.
How could she tell the time?
But if one of the nuns
kept me after
to wash the blackboard
and clap erasers
for talking out of line,
Jonsey would walk the length
of Fifth to Broad Street,
red rubber ball in her mouth,
and wait for the 3:45
to drop me
at the main entrance
to Cedar Grove Cemetery
where she'd drop
the ball at my feet,
furiously wagging her tail,
waiting for the first toss

as we playfully made
our way home,

neither of us worried
about time.

The Other

Into our backyard
came the black Manx
unopposed
for the first time,
sniffing dirt
about the azalea
we planted
over our old calico
who gave no quarter
before her kidneys
gave out.

The Manx
watched me in the glass
of our patio door
or perhaps caught only
his own crafty self
given back, each ear
tracking on its own,
his gaze
snapping to.

Then he sprayed
the azalea
and tensed for trouble
that kept not coming.
One slow step
after another,
as if weakened
by this final yellow
of a feud
lasting years,
he disappeared
for the last time.

Claws and Wings

That last year in college we drank our way
              toward diplomas at the lobster pound
where Crowley, the alky owner and non-
              stop talker, always needed an audience.
I can still see them ghosting in green water,
              us watching—Bill, Ray, and me, but rarely
Joe who kept his afternoons a secret for months.

At Biddeford Pool in our beachfront rental
              we'd sip coffee and watch the sun rise
out of the ocean before heading to class.
              Sometimes storms entertained. Buoys
and traps once tumbled in the surf. We hauled
              them above the tide line, a favor
to the boatmen, then helped ourselves
              to lobsters that would have died anyway—
or so our reasoning went. Joe donned
              a chef's hat for once. Dozens of claws
clicked on our kitchen floor waiting for kettles
              to boil like tempers when we
competed for a few pale nurses from Portland.

But Joe was absent at party time too—
              flying lessons, we learned at last, and
restoring a Piper Cub he bought on the cheap
              while we were drinking down stories
at the pound, old Crowley's face getting red
              as a boiled claw, slurring about Nazis . . .
pointing to some crate wood stenciled in German
              that hung from an overhead beam . . .
A U-boat just off the beach before dawn.
              Eight kraut spies in two rubber rafts rowed in,
buried the rafts, and headed for Boston—

all caught, tried, and shot by firing squad.
Look it up, said Crowley. I <u>did</u>. It <u>happened</u>.

Grumman Avengers were scrambled from Pease
      and dive-bombed the sub before it could find
deep water . . . You could hear and feel the thuds.
      That night I told Joe how debris, like that piece
of crate, washed up with the tide and how Crowley
      passed out at the end. Ray unpegged a few
claws and we watched them lock on each other,
      Crowley slumped in his chair, mouth open,
Bill's *Playboy* pillowing his head for laughs.

Joe wasn't there either for the Friday night
      party-girl follies, my fistfight with Bill,
the broken mirror and lamp, or hungover
      Sundays with football players bunched
and locked in the small pound of our black-
      and-white TV. The yellow Cub finished,
solo license in hand, Joe buzzed our house
      that spring—us looking up, waving—
and later told me, with a huge smile, that flying
      was *a dream controlled.* I can still see
his room, bed made, blanket taut, closet open
      as if for inspection, shoes buffed to a mirror
and placed just so, the latest issue of *Wings*
      or *Flying* on his uncluttered desk.

Ray made his way into real estate,
      banking for Bill, teaching for me.
And Joe? In an F-4 Phantom, he exploded
      over Hanoi. His dream out of control
has me seeing lobsters again ghosting
      in the green water, unpegged, locked
on each other, like parts of the past
      waiting for my fingers to sort them.

Letter to Bill Heyen

The 9/11 Anthology

I never said thanks for the invitation
to write something, but nothing
would come, nothing but the paralyzing image
of that office worker in midair, a man,
his necktie pointing up

toward the window he leaped from.
I was a hostage to moods: anger and sadness,
the typical swings. Mostly I was numb, sometimes
even envious of faces twisted and crying on television news.
Almost four months later, I'm in Sun Devil Stadium.

Not quite wanting to be, I'm at the Fiesta Bowl
with a family of in-laws and friends—
all hardcore fans but me. I'm beginning to seethe,
thinking about football—the tail that wags a university,
the academic slack that's cut for jocks,

the cynical coaches, the scholar-athlete charade,
the whole sleazy business
that grows in sync with our addiction to sports.
Anyway, I'm sitting there with this anger,
feeling like Malvolio among the happy fans,

their faces painted with bison and ducks.
But I'm nervous too
because it's that same kind of perfect day,
sunny and blue, and passenger jets are low overhead
on their last leg into Sky Harbor just west of us.

I try to focus on pregame pass drills and warm-ups
when six Air Force skydivers exit

a de Havilland prop from ten thousand feet,
their canopies yellow, green, and white.
With binocs I watch them tack and spiral in.

Each one tries for the red rectangle at midfield.
The last diver trails a big rippling flag,
the Stars and Stripes,
and nails the target. My breath catches,
everything blurs. I'm choking back sobs,

eyes wet behind sunglasses I'm glad to be wearing
when an Apache gunship roars over the stadium,
and my right arm lifts on its own, my hand a fist.
I whisper *Yes.* I can barely believe it.
But others too, sniffling, handkerchiefs out.

A Mexican guy with a mustache, his cheeks
shiny with tears. The woman next to me,
touching Kleenex to her face, takes my arm.
Suddenly, after months, I'm at the sorrow of Ground Zero
with a deep sense of the team I belong to.

Valéry was right: we're locked outside ourselves.
Which is why poems exist. Something in me
wanted out, I found the right key, and it finally emerged,
but late, Bill, too late for the book. Sorry I couldn't deliver.

Matins

A curve of beach, a moon,
    Hunter leaning overhead,
       Surf all slam and seethe.
    I move closer to the lights
Of two barges and a tug at anchor

A hundred yards off the bar—
    A demonic factory
Pumping back sand
    That's been taken by storms.
I'm walking with the hard news:

Your wife and daughter on the first plane,
    A friend on the second,
Those undying fiery towers.
    Diesels drone on the barges,
Increasing store with loss

And loss with store—an old line
    Against an edge under siege.
Dark figures move on the decks.
    I turn away, listen to the surf's
White noise, salt on my lips,

Walk until I'm sleepy again,
    Stars fading in the east, a call
For prayers, chanting voices
    Lighter than this foam
Blown along the hard wet sand.

Breath

We die of words—Ralph Waldo Emerson

Their echoes eddy,
vanish, and endlessly want more.
But once I quietly inflated two blue air pallets
for the children of visiting friends
and like to remember that night
when held lightly above our hardwood floor
they floated toward dreams
on my breath.

Last Day on the Island

I must have known.
Small craft warnings were up.
On our cottage deck,
the Blue Devils flag was tattering
to shreds on the owner's pole.

I urged my father to take my arm—
a walk on the soft sand would help.
After a few minutes, he stopped.
I stepped back
to take this picture—his eyes wrinkled
like those of dwindling loggerheads
that weeks ago
made it out into the open water.

But this is double exposure: me
watching him
earlier that week
as he entered the easier waves
on stick legs, got smaller
and smaller
until I
thought he
would vanish completely.

The camera was a box
made of my fingers, a gag
to lift us into laughter.
Now I have him
still standing on his own
before the toppling waves,
in his blue slicker, electric
blue as the moment,

laughing,
giving form to the infinite
depth of field
at his back.

Après le Déluge, *or How to Return*

Forget the French fads,
Foucault, Sartre, and Derrida,
paradigms, the eggistential toothpick,
the semiotic egg, and the text
beyond which there is nothing
but eggheads.

Make the river your own. Rename it the Tar
after its shiny blackness and nothing will fall
routinely into place
like that dogwood, white and dying
for attention at your window.

Tell yourself a room's the wrong place to receive.
Quit the house like a bad job.
Hand your dead brother the shovel,
shove off in a leaky canoe
and follow that Monarch—its orange wings
          flit above the current.
Immensity will make a return
and every face will offer less
than the smooth cool face of the water.

Let the river teach you
how to steer toward subtle surprise.
Tell me, what even comes close
to this scented air you've noticed for the first time?

The sun falls,
anoints the surface with orange oil.
Dark lifts from the water faster than you think.
A meander brings
a soft snicker of owl wings close to your gunnels.

Around the bend, a lamp appears
with a Coleman hiss
and a hunched figure with his hook,
shaped like a question, pole-tossed in the current.

That's it, that's it.
Everything you need
is beginning to find you.

Acknowledgments

Grateful acknowledgment is made to editors of the following publications in which some of these poems or earlier versions of them first appeared:

Anglican Theological Review: "Wisteria" and "In Advent Dark";
Blackbird: "Après le Déluge, or How to Return";
Chariton Review: "Barrier Island" and "After Hurricane Earl";
Connotation Press: "Gone";
Cumberland River Review: "Developing Story";
Ecotone: "Nightcatch";
Epoch: "Mandatory Evacuation, Late August";
The Gettysburg Review: "Notes" and "The Other";
The Hampden-Sydney Review: "Jumping Mullet";
The Hudson Review: "Claws and Wings" and "Power Outage";
Iodine Poetry Journal: "Parish School";
Kestrel: "Letter to Bill Heyen";
The Louisville Review: "Petunias on the Deck," "Towhees and Late Light," and "Now";
The Nation: "Streetlamps";
The News & Observer: Arts and Leisure: "Tennis Courts in December" and "Flu Days";
North American Review: "Roadside";
North Carolina Literary Review: "Night Passage" and "Practice";
One: "Last Day on the Island";
Potomac Review: "Names";
Prairie Schooner: "Fixative";
Seminary Ridge Review: "Blue Beyond Black and White";
The Sewanee Review: "Out of Range," "Mother's Day," "Coastal Java Shack," "Orthodox Priest," and "Miss Jones";
Southern Poetry Review: "Matins," "Outer Banks Nightlife," "Picnic near St. Rémy";
The Southern Review: "Breath";
Tar River Poetry: "Tattoo," "What Color Does," "Footstool and Mug," and "Yellow Chair in the Dunes";

West Branch: "Burro at Christmas."

"Signs" was published in a chapbook entitled *Back Roads* (Independent Press, 2009).

"Winter" was published in *The Store of Joys: Writers Celebrate the North Carolina Museum of Art's Fiftieth Anniversary* (John F. Blair, Publisher, 1997).

"Canyonlands in October" and "The Route" were published in *Southern Poetry Anthology,* Volume VII (Texas Review Press, 2014).

⁕

"Orthodox Priest" is for Everett Thomas.

"After Hurricane Earl" is for Mark Brazaitis.

"Canyonlands in October" is for Susan and Cless.

"Matins" is in memory of my friend David McCourt, and his family.

Finally, I would like to express my thanks to Peter Conners for his careful editing and excellent suggestions for revision.

About the Author

Peter Makuck is a Distinguished Professor Emeritus at East Carolina University, where he founded and edited *Tar River Poetry* for almost thirty years. In 2008 he was Lee Smith Visiting Poet at North Carolina State University. He has also been a visiting writer at Brigham Young University and University of North Carolina at Wilmington. His stories, poems, reviews, and essays have appeared in *Poetry, The Nation, The Georgia Review, The Hudson Review, The Gettysburg Review*, and *The Sewanee Review*. In addition to five previous volumes of poems, five poetry chapbooks, and three collections of short stories, he has co-edited a book of essays, *An Open World*, on the Welsh poet Leslie Norris. His most recent collection of short stories is *Allegiance and Betrayal* (Syracuse University Press, 2013). *Long Lens: New & Selected Poems*, also published by BOA Editions, was released in 2010 and won the Brockman-Campbell Award (given annually for the best collection of poetry by a North Carolinian). Former Fulbright Exchange Professor to France and recipient of the Charity Randall Citation from the International Poetry Forum, he lives with his wife Phyllis on Bogue Banks, one of North Carolina's barrier islands.

✳

BOA Editions, Ltd.
American Poets Continuum Series

Colophon

BOA Editions, Ltd., a not-for-profit publisher of poetry and other literary works, fosters readership and appreciation of contemporary literature. By identifying, cultivating, and publishing both new and established poets and selecting authors of unique literary talent, BOA brings high-quality literature to the public. Support for this effort comes from the sale of its publications, grant funding, and private donations.

✳

The publication of this book is made possible, in part,
by the support of the following patrons:

Anonymous
Gwen & Gary Conners
Steven O. Russell & Phyllis Rifkin-Russell

and the kind sponsorship of the following individuals:

Anonymous x 2
Nin Andrews
Nickole Brown & Jessica Jacobs
Bernadette Catalana
Christopher & DeAnna Cebula
Anne C. Coon & Craig J. Zicari
Jere Fletcher
Michael Hall, *in memory of Lorna Hall*
Sandi Henschel, *in honor of my friend Boo Poulin*
Grant Holcomb
Christopher Kennedy & Mi Ditmar
X. J. & Dorothy M. Kennedy
Keetje Kuipers & Sarah Fritsch, *in memory of JoAnn Wood Graham*
Jack & Gail Langerak
Daniel M. Meyers, *in honor of James Shepard Skiff*
Deborah Ronnen & Sherman Levey
Sue S. Stewart, *in memory of Stephen L. Raymond*
Lynda & George Waldrep
Michael Waters & Mihaela Moscaliuc
Michael & Patricia Wilder